times tables

Text: Nina Filipek
and Sheila and Ian Spence

Published in Great Britain by World International Publishing Limited,
an Egmont Company, Egmont House,
PO Box III, Great Ducie Street,
Manchester M60 3BL.

Printed in Finland.
ISBN 0 7498 0653 2

A catalogue record for this book is available from the British Library.

To the student

In this book you will find the times tables from 2 to 10. Learn to say the tables by repeating them over and over again. Study the hundred squares and notice the patterns the numbers make. Try to answer the questions based on the tables. Then go on to practise multiplication exercises. Read through the examples carefully and try to answer the questions. The calculations are easy to start with, then become more difficult. Check your results with the answers at the back of the book.

Counting in twos

This is a table of twos.

1	2	3	4	5	6	7	8	9	10
11	12	13	14	15	16	17	18	19	20
21	22	23	24	25	26	27	28	29	30
31	32	33	34	35	36	37	38	39	40
41	42	43	44	45	46	47	48	49	50
51	52	53	54	55	56	57	58	59	60
61	62	63	64	65	66	67	68	69	70
71	72	73	74	75	76	77	78	79	80
81	82	83	84	85	86	87	88	89	90
91	92	93	94	95	96	97	98	99	100

Learn to count in twos. Starting from 2 at the top of the square, and reading across, repeat out loud the numbers you see in the coloured boxes. Notice the pattern in the order of the numbers.

0	×	2	=	**0**
1	×	2	=	**2**
2	×	2	=	**4**
3	×	2	=	**6**
4	×	2	=	**8**
5	×	2	=	**10**
6	×	2	=	**12**
7	×	2	=	**14**
8	×	2	=	**16**
9	×	2	=	**18**
10	×	2	=	**20**
11	×	2	=	**22**
12	×	2	=	**24**

Now try these!

Count forwards in twos, filling in the missing numbers.

Example:

2, 4, 6, [8] [10] [12]

1. 14, 16, 18, [20] [22] [24]

2. 80, 82, [84] [86] [88] [90]

3. 34, 36, 38, [40] [42] [44]

4. 58, [60] [62] 64, [66] [68]

5. 22, 24, [26] [28] [30] [32]

Complete the sums.

Example:

9 × 2 = 18

1.	10	×	2	=	20
2.	6	×	2	=	12
3.	4	×	2	=	8
4.	12	×	2	=	24
5.	8	×	2	=	16

How many did you get right?

Check your answers.

Counting in threes

This is a table of threes.

1	2	3	4	5	6	7	8	9	10
11	12	13	14	15	16	17	18	19	20
21	22	23	24	25	26	27	28	29	30
31	32	33	34	35	36	37	38	39	40
41	42	43	44	45	46	47	48	49	50
51	52	53	54	55	56	57	58	59	60
61	62	63	64	65	66	67	68	69	70
71	72	73	74	75	76	77	78	79	80
81	82	83	84	85	86	87	88	89	90
91	92	93	94	95	96	97	98	99	100

Learn to count in threes.

Try counting backwards, too.

0	×	3	=	**0**
1	×	3	=	**3**
2	×	3	=	**6**
3	×	3	=	**9**
4	×	3	=	**12**
5	×	3	=	**15**
6	×	3	=	**18**
7	×	3	=	**21**
8	×	3	=	**24**
9	×	3	=	**27**
10	×	3	=	**30**
11	×	3	=	**33**
12	×	3	=	**36**

Now try these!

Count backwards in threes, filling in the missing numbers.

Example:

36, 33, 30, [27] [24] [21]

1. 18, 15, 12, [9] [6] [3]

2. 39, 36, 33, [30] [27] [24]

3. 78, 75, [72] [69] [66] [63]

4. 66, [63] [60] [56] [53]

5. 45, 42, [48] [45] [42]

Write the answers only.

Example:

$4 \times 3 = $ 12

1. $6 \times 3 = $ 18
2. $2 \times 3 = $ 6
3. $11 \times 3 = $ 33
4. $9 \times 3 = $ 27
5. $10 \times 3 = $ 30

How well did you do this time?

Counting in fours

This is a table of fours.

1	2	3	4	5	6	7	8	9	10
11	12	13	14	15	16	17	18	19	20
21	22	23	24	25	26	27	28	29	30
31	32	33	34	35	36	37	38	39	40
41	42	43	44	45	46	47	48	49	50
51	52	53	54	55	56	57	58	59	60
61	62	63	64	65	66	67	68	69	70
71	72	73	74	75	76	77	78	79	80
81	82	83	84	85	86	87	88	89	90
91	92	93	94	95	96	97	98	99	100

Try counting in fours.
Use the table to help you.

0	×	4	=	**0**
1	×	4	=	**4**
2	×	4	=	**8**
3	×	4	=	**12**
4	×	4	=	**16**
5	×	4	=	**20**
6	×	4	=	**24**
7	×	4	=	**28**
8	×	4	=	**32**
9	×	4	=	**36**
10	×	4	=	**40**
11	×	4	=	**44**
12	×	4	=	**48**

Now try these!

Complete the sums.

1.	1	×	4	=	4
2.	4	×	4	=	16
3.	10	×	4	=	40
4.	12	×	4	=	48
5.	7	×	4	=	28
6.	12	×	4	=	48
7.	0	×	4	=	0
8.	6	×	4	=	24
9.	9	×	4	=	36
10.	8	×	4	=	32

Write the answers only.

Example:

$$\begin{array}{r} 4 \\ \times 4 \\ \hline 16 \end{array}$$

1. $$\begin{array}{r} 5 \\ \times 4 \\ \hline \square \end{array}$$

2. $$\begin{array}{r} 8 \\ \times 4 \\ \hline \square \end{array}$$

3. $$\begin{array}{r} 12 \\ \times 4 \\ \hline \square \end{array}$$

4. $$\begin{array}{r} 11 \\ \times 4 \\ \hline \square \end{array}$$

5. $$\begin{array}{r} 1 \\ \times 4 \\ \hline \square \end{array}$$

Check your answers and correct any mistakes.

Counting in fives

This is a table of fives.

1	2	3	4	5	6	7	8	9	10
11	12	13	14	15	16	17	18	19	20
21	22	23	24	25	26	27	28	29	30
31	32	33	34	35	36	37	38	39	40
41	42	43	44	45	46	47	48	49	50
51	52	53	54	55	56	57	58	59	60
61	62	63	64	65	66	67	68	69	70
71	72	73	74	75	76	77	78	79	80
81	82	83	84	85	86	87	88	89	90
91	92	93	94	95	96	97	98	99	100

Count backwards
in fives using
the table
to help you.

0	×	5	=	**0**
1	×	5	=	**5**
2	×	5	=	**10**
3	×	5	=	**15**
4	×	5	=	**20**
5	×	5	=	**25**
6	×	5	=	**30**
7	×	5	=	**35**
8	×	5	=	**40**
9	×	5	=	**45**
10	×	5	=	**50**
11	×	5	=	**55**
12	×	5	=	**60**

Now try these!

Read the following questions carefully and write the answer in the box.

Example:

How many fives in 50?

Answer: 50 = [10] fives

1. How many fives in 40?

   Answer: 40 = [8] fives

2. How many fives in 25?

   Answer: 25 = [ ] fives

3. How many fives in 45?

   Answer: 45 = [ ] fives

4. How many fives in 60?

   Answer: 60 = [ ] fives

5. How many fives in 20?

   Answer: 20 = [ ] fives

Write the answers only.

Work as quickly as you can.

1.	6	×	5	=	☐
2.	8	×	5	=	☐
3.	11	×	5	=	☐
4.	0	×	5	=	☐
5.	3	×	5	=	☐

Easy, wasn't it?

Counting in sixes

This is a table of sixes.

1	2	3	4	5	6	7	8	9	10
11	12	13	14	15	16	17	18	19	20
21	22	23	24	25	26	27	28	29	30
31	32	33	34	35	36	37	38	39	40
41	42	43	44	45	46	47	48	49	50
51	52	53	54	55	56	57	58	59	60
61	62	63	64	65	66	67	68	69	70
71	72	73	74	75	76	77	78	79	80
81	82	83	84	85	86	87	88	89	90
91	92	93	94	95	96	97	98	99	100

1898+5005=

Can you count in sixes?

6903.000

0	×	6	=	**0**
1	×	6	=	**6**
2	×	6	=	**12**
3	×	6	=	**18**
4	×	6	=	**24**
5	×	6	=	**30**
6	×	6	=	**36**
7	×	6	=	**42**
8	×	6	=	**48**
9	×	6	=	**54**
10	×	6	=	**60**
11	×	6	=	**66**
12	×	6	=	**72**

Now try these!

Complete the sums.

Example:

2 × 6 = **6** × 2

1. 1 × 6 = ☐ × 1
2. 3 × 6 = ☐ × 3
3. 0 × 6 = ☐ × 0
4. 5 × 6 = ☐ × 5
5. 4 × 6 = ☐ × 4
6. ☐ × 6 = 6 × 7
7. ☐ × 6 = 6 × 10
8. ☐ × 6 = 6 × 9
9. ☐ × 6 = 6 × 8
10. ☐ × 6 = 6 × 12

Write the answers only.

1. $8 \times 6 = \square$

$6 \times 8 = \square$

2. $3 \times 6 = \square$

$6 \times 3 = \square$

3. $10 \times 6 = \square$

$6 \times 10 = \square$

4. $4 \times 6 = \square$

$6 \times 4 = \square$

5. $12 \times 6 = \square$

$6 \times 12 = \square$

How many did you get right?

Check your answers.

Counting in sevens.

This is a table of sevens.

1	2	3	4	5	6	7	8	9	10
11	12	13	14	15	16	17	18	19	20
21	22	23	24	25	26	27	28	29	30
31	32	33	34	35	36	37	38	39	40
41	42	43	44	45	46	47	48	49	50
51	52	53	54	55	56	57	58	59	60
61	62	63	64	65	66	67	68	69	70
71	72	73	74	75	76	77	78	79	80
81	82	83	84	85	86	87	88	89	90
91	92	93	94	95	96	97	98	99	100

Learn to count
in sevens up to 49.

Use the table to help you.

0	×	7	=	**0**
1	×	7	=	**7**
2	×	7	=	**14**
3	×	7	=	**21**
4	×	7	=	**28**
5	×	7	=	**35**
6	×	7	=	**42**
7	×	7	=	**49**
8	×	7	=	**56**
9	×	7	=	**63**
10	×	7	=	**70**
11	×	7	=	**77**
12	×	7	=	**84**

Now try these!

Here is some speed practice.

Complete the following noting the time you start and the time you finish.

1.	6	×	6	=	☐
2.	7	×	3	=	☐
3.	3	×	☐	=	6
4.	4	×	4	=	☐
5.	6	×	☐	=	24
6.	7	×	7	=	☐
7.	3	×	☐	=	9

8. $4 \times 5 = \square$

9. $7 \times \square = 42$

10. $10 \times \square = 50$

11. $25 = \square$ fives

12. $0 \times 6 = \square$

13. $3 \times 8 = \square$

14. $7 \times \square = 14$

15. $$\begin{array}{r} 12 \\ \times 4 \\ \hline \square \end{array}$$

If you finished the sums in less than ten minutes and got them all right – well done! If not – you need to learn your tables.

Counting in eights

This is a table of eights.

1	2	3	4	5	6	7	8	9	10
11	12	13	14	15	16	17	18	19	20
21	22	23	24	25	26	27	28	29	30
31	32	33	34	35	36	37	38	39	40
41	42	43	44	45	46	47	48	49	50
51	52	53	54	55	56	57	58	59	60
61	62	63	64	65	66	67	68	69	70
71	72	73	74	75	76	77	78	79	80
81	82	83	84	85	86	87	88	89	90
91	92	93	94	95	96	97	98	99	100

Compare it to the table of fours on page 12.
What do you notice?

0	×	8	=	**0**
1	×	8	=	**8**
2	×	8	=	**16**
3	×	8	=	**24**
4	×	8	=	**32**
5	×	8	=	**40**
6	×	8	=	**48**
7	×	8	=	**56**
8	×	8	=	**64**
9	×	8	=	**72**
10	×	8	=	**80**
11	×	8	=	**88**
12	×	8	=	**96**

Now try these!

Complete the sums.

1.	0	×	8	=	☐
2.	4	×	8	=	☐
3.	7	×	8	=	☐
4.	5	×	8	=	☐
5.	12	×	8	=	☐
6.	8	×	☐	=	64
7.	☐	×	8	=	0
8.	10	×	☐	=	80
9.	☐	×	8	=	88
10.	3	×	☐	=	24

Write the answers only.

1. $\begin{array}{r} 6 \\ \times 8 \\ \hline \square \end{array}$

2. $\begin{array}{r} 0 \\ \times 8 \\ \hline \square \end{array}$

3. $\begin{array}{r} 9 \\ \times 8 \\ \hline \square \end{array}$

4. $\begin{array}{r} 12 \\ \times 8 \\ \hline \square \end{array}$

5. $\begin{array}{r} 10 \\ \times 8 \\ \hline \square \end{array}$

Now check your answers.

Counting in nines

This is a table of nines.

1	2	3	4	5	6	7	8	9	10
11	12	13	14	15	16	17	18	19	20
21	22	23	24	25	26	27	28	29	30
31	32	33	34	35	36	37	38	39	40
41	42	43	44	45	46	47	48	49	50
51	52	53	54	55	56	57	58	59	60
61	62	63	64	65	66	67	68	69	70
71	72	73	74	75	76	77	78	79	80
81	82	83	84	85	86	87	88	89	90
91	92	93	94	95	96	97	98	99	100

Learn to count in nines.

Notice that the numbers form a diagonal pattern.

Compare this with the table of threes on page 8.

0	×	9	=	**0**
1	×	9	=	**9**
2	×	9	=	**18**
3	×	9	=	**27**
4	×	9	=	**36**
5	×	9	=	**45**
6	×	9	=	**54**
7	×	9	=	**63**
8	×	9	=	**72**
9	×	9	=	**81**
10	×	9	=	**90**
11	×	9	=	**99**
12	×	9	=	**108**

Now try these!

Fill in the missing numbers by counting forwards or backwards in nines.

(See the examples on pages 6 and 10.)

1. 0, 9, ☐ ☐ ☐

2. 54, ☐ ☐ 81

3. 81, ☐ ☐ 54

4. ☐ 9, ☐ ☐

5. ☐ 36, ☐ ☐ ☐

Write the answers only.

(See example on page 15.)

1. $5 \times 9 = \square$

2. $9 \times 9 = \square$

3. $3 \times 9 = \square$

4. $6 \times 9 = \square$

5. $11 \times 9 = \square$

Check your answers.

Counting in tens

This is a table of tens.

1	2	3	4	5	6	7	8	9	10
11	12	13	14	15	16	17	18	19	20
21	22	23	24	25	26	27	28	29	30
31	32	33	34	35	36	37	38	39	40
41	42	43	44	45	46	47	48	49	50
51	52	53	54	55	56	57	58	59	60
61	62	63	64	65	66	67	68	69	70
71	72	73	74	75	76	77	78	79	80
81	82	83	84	85	86	87	88	89	90
91	92	93	94	95	96	97	98	99	100

Learn to count forwards and backwards in tens.

0	×	10	=	**0**
1	×	10	=	**10**
2	×	10	=	**20**
3	×	10	=	**30**
4	×	10	=	**40**
5	×	10	=	**50**
6	×	10	=	**60**
7	×	10	=	**70**
8	×	10	=	**80**
9	×	10	=	**90**
10	×	10	=	**100**
11	×	10	=	**110**
12	×	10	=	**120**

Now try these!

Complete the sums.

1.	100	=	10	tens
2.	70	=	7	tens
3.	50	=	5	tens
4.	30	=	3	tens
5.	80	=	8	tens
6.	6 tens	=	60	
7.	9 tens	=	90	
8.	11 tens	=	[illegible]	
9.	12 tens	=	120	
10.	4 tens	=	40	

Fill in the missing numbers by counting forwards or backwards in tens.

1. 0, 10, [20] [30]

2. 60, [70] 80, [90]

3. 100, [110] [120] [130] 60

4. [50] 60, 70, [80] [90]

5. [10] [20] [30] 40, 50

Now check your answers.

Multiplication is easy if you know your tables!

The sign $\times$ means 'is multiplied by'.

You can check your multiplication by repeated addition.

Example:

$$9 \times 3 = 27$$

$$\begin{array}{r} 9 \\ \times 3 \\ \hline 27 \end{array}$$

$$\begin{array}{r} 0 \\ +9 \\ \boxed{9} \\ +9 \\ \boxed{18} \\ +9 \\ \boxed{27} \end{array}$$

Note: 9×3 is 3 lots of 9, or 9 times 3.

Examples: 10 × 4 = 40

$$\begin{array}{r} 10 \\ \times\ 4 \\ \hline 40 \end{array}$$

0
+10
10
+10
20
+10
30
+10
40

$$\begin{array}{r} 6 \\ \times\ 5 \\ \hline 30 \end{array}$$

6 × 5 = 30

0
+6
6
+6
12
+6
18
+6
24
+6
30

Now do these:

1. a $3 \times 4 = \square$

   0

   +3

   b $\square$

   +3

   c $\square$

   +3

   d $\square$

   +3

   e $\square$

2. a $8 \times 5 = \square$

   0

   +8

   b $\square$

   +8

   c $\square$

   +8

   d $\square$

   +8

   e $\square$

   +8

   f $\square$

3. a $9 \times 3 = \square$

b $0 + 9 = \square$

c $+9 = \square$

d $+9 = \square$

4. a $7 \times 4 = \square$

b $0 + 7 = \square$

c $+7 = \square$

d $+7 = \square$

e $+7 = \square$

1. a $12 \times 6 =$ ☐

b
$$\begin{array}{r} 12 \\ \times 6 \\ \hline \square \end{array}$$

2. a $11 \times 5 =$ ☐

b
$$\begin{array}{r} 11 \\ \times 5 \\ \hline \square \end{array}$$

3. a $7 \times 8 =$ ☐

b
$$\begin{array}{r} 7 \\ \times 8 \\ \hline \square \end{array}$$

4. a $8 \times 3 =$ ☐

b
$$\begin{array}{r} 8 \\ \times 3 \\ \hline \square \end{array}$$

Now check your answers.

1. 0

+ 12
a ☐
+ 12
b ☐
+ 12
c ☐
+ 12
d ☐
+ 12
e ☐
+ 12
f ☐

2. 0

+ 11
a ☐
+ 11
b ☐
+ 11
c ☐
+ 11
d ☐
+ 11
e ☐

3. 0

+ 7
a ☐
+ 7
b ☐
+ 7
c ☐
+ 7
d ☐
+ 7
e ☐
+ 7
f ☐
+ 7
g ☐
+ 7
h ☐

4. 0

+ 8
a ☐
+ 8
b ☐
+ 8
c ☐

Remember!

4×5 and 5×4 give the same answer.

1. 0

+4

a ☐

+4

b ☐

+4

c ☐

+4

d ☐

+4

e ☐

3. 0

+5

a ☐

+5

b ☐

+5

c ☐

+5

d ☐

2. 4

×5

☐

4. 5

×4

☐

Try these:

7 × 5 and 5 × 7

1.

0
+7
a ☐
+7
b ☐
+7
c ☐
+7
d ☐
+7
e ☐

3.

0
+5
a ☐
+5
b ☐
+5
c ☐
+5
d ☐
+5
e ☐
+5
f ☐
+5
g ☐

2.

7
× 5
☐

4.

5
× 7
☐

A multiplication square is very helpful.

×	1	2	3	4	5	6	7	8	9	10
1	1	2	3	4	5	6	7	8	9	10
2	2	4	6	8	10	12	14	16	18	20
3	3	6	9	12	15	18	21	24	27	30
4	4	8	12	16	20	24	28	32	36	40
5	5	10	15	20	25	30	35	40	45	50
6	6	12	18	24	30	36	42	48	54	60
7	7	14	21	28	35	42	49	56	63	70
8	8	16	24	32	40	48	56	64	72	80
9	9	18	27	36	45	54	63	72	81	90
10	10	20	30	40	50	60	70	80	90	100

Using the multiplication square.

Example: 8 × 7 = 56

First, find 8 in the first column on the left.

Move your finger along the 8 row until you are **under** the 7 in the top row.

What is the number in the square where your finger is?

Yes, it should be 56.

Find these:

1. 4 × 2 = ☐

2. 2 × 4 = ☐

3. 9 × 6 = ☐

4. 4 × 7 = ☐

Check your answers.

Now do these:

1.	2	×	7	=	☐
2.	5	×	☐	=	20
3.	☐	×	7	=	49
4.	☐	×	3	=	15
5.	8	×	☐	=	16
6.	☐	×	9	=	36
7.	8	×	5	=	☐
8.	3	×	☐	=	6
9.	9	×	3	=	☐
10.	☐	×	6	=	42
11.	7	×	9	=	☐
12.	6	×	☐	=	6

1. $\begin{array}{r} 12 \\ \times 7 \\ \hline \square \end{array}$

2. $\begin{array}{r} 9 \\ \times 1 \\ \hline \square \end{array}$

3. $\begin{array}{r} 11 \\ \times 10 \\ \hline \square \end{array}$

4. $\begin{array}{r} 3 \\ \times 4 \\ \hline \square \end{array}$

5. $\begin{array}{r} 7 \\ \times 5 \\ \hline \square \end{array}$

6. $\begin{array}{r} 8 \\ \times 3 \\ \hline \square \end{array}$

7. $\begin{array}{r} 6 \\ \times 2 \\ \hline \square \end{array}$

8. $\begin{array}{r} 3 \\ \times 8 \\ \hline \square \end{array}$

9. $\begin{array}{r} 10 \\ \times 8 \\ \hline \square \end{array}$

10. $\begin{array}{r} 9 \\ \times 9 \\ \hline \square \end{array}$

Now check your answers.

Example:

$$\begin{array}{r} 12 \\ \times 5 \\ \hline 60 \end{array}$$

This can be done by writing

$10 \times 5 = 50$

and $2 \times 5 = 10$

Add the two answers to make the total = 60.

Do this one:

1. a

$$\begin{array}{r} 11 \\ \times 7 \\ \hline \square \end{array}$$

b $10 \times 7 = \square$

c $1 \times 7 = \square$

d Total $= \square$

Check your answers.

Now do these:

1. $\begin{array}{r} 12 \\ \times 10 \\ \hline \end{array}$

a ☐

b 10 × 10 = ☐

c 2 × 10 = ☐

d Total = ☐

2. $\begin{array}{r} 15 \\ \times 9 \\ \hline \end{array}$

a ☐

b 10 × 9 = ☐

c 5 × 9 = ☐

d Total = ☐

3. $\begin{array}{r} 21 \\ \times 8 \\ \hline \end{array}$

a ☐

b 10 × 8 = ☐

c 10 × 8 = ☐

d 1 × 8 = ☐

e Total = ☐

There is an easier way of writing multiplications.

Example:

$$\begin{array}{r} 24 \\ \times 6 \\ \hline 144 \\ \hline {\scriptstyle 2} \end{array}$$

We start with the units:

$$4 \times 6 = 24$$

Write the 4 units in the answer space. Carry the 2 tens to be added to the answer later.
Multiply the tens:

$$2 \text{ tens} \times 6 = 12 \text{ tens}$$

Add the 2 tens carried from the units:

$$12 \text{ tens} + 2 \text{ tens} = 14 \text{ tens}$$

And write 14 in the answer space.

Do these:

1. 17 × 5 = ☐

2. 15 × 6 = ☐

3. 24 × 8 = ☐

4. 26 × 9 = ☐

5. 18 × 9 = ☐

6. 33 × 4 = ☐

7. 39 × 8 = ☐

8. 42 × 7 = ☐

9. 83 × 5 = ☐

10. 76 × 7 = ☐

You can now multiply some larger numbers.

Example:

$$\begin{array}{r} 153 \\ \times\ 5 \\ \hline 765 \\ \hline {\scriptstyle 2\ 1} \end{array}$$

This can be done by writing

$$100 \times 5 = 500$$
$$50 \times 5 = 250$$
$$3 \times 5 = 15$$
$$\text{Total} = 765$$

You can check this by adding:

$$\begin{array}{r} 0 \\ +\,153 \\ \boxed{153} \\ +\,153 \\ \boxed{306} \\ +\,153 \\ \boxed{459} \\ +\,153 \\ \boxed{612} \\ +\,153 \\ \boxed{765} \end{array}$$

$$153 \times 5 = 765$$

Now do these and check them on a piece of paper using repeated addition.

1. 124 × 3 = ☐

2. 167 × 5 = ☐

3. 199 × 8 = ☐

4. 205 × 6 = ☐

5. 316 × 4 = ☐

6. 178 × 9 = ☐

7. 422 × 8 = ☐

8. 547 × 7 = ☐

9. 215 × 10 = ☐

10. 644 × 2 = ☐

Example:

$$\begin{array}{r} 184 \\ \times\ 9 \\ \hline 1656 \\ \hline {\scriptstyle 7\ 3} \end{array}$$

This can be done by writing

$100 \times 9 = 900$

$80 \times 9 = 720$

$4 \times 9 = 36$

$184 \times 9 = 1656$

Do this one:

1.

$$\begin{array}{r} 257 \\ \times 8 \\ \hline \end{array}$$

a ☐

b $200 \times 8 =$ ☐

c $50 \times 8 =$ ☐

d $7 \times 8 =$ ☐

e Total = ☐

f $257 \times 8 =$ ☐

Do these in the same way.

1.

$$\begin{array}{r} 396 \\ \times\ 7 \\ \hline \end{array}$$

a ☐

b 300 × 7 = ☐

c 90 × 7 = ☐

d 6 × 7 = ☐

e Total = ☐

f 396 × 7 = ☐

2.

$$\begin{array}{r} 278 \\ \times\ 10 \\ \hline \end{array}$$

a ☐

b 200 × 10 = ☐

c 70 × 10 = ☐

d 8 × 10 = ☐

e Total = ☐

f 278 × 10 = ☐

Looking back:

Complete these multiplications.

1.	2	×	3	=	☐
2.	8	×	7	=	☐
3.	11	×	9	=	☐
4.	7	×	☐	=	42
5.	6	×	☐	=	48
6.	12	×	10	=	☐
7.	☐	×	3	=	36
8.	☐	×	7	=	49
9.	5	×	8	=	☐
10.	12	×	9	=	☐

1. $6 \times 1 =$ ☐

2. $4 \times 2 =$ ☐

3. $6 \times 3 =$ ☐

4. $9 \times 8 =$ ☐

5. $12 \times 9 =$ ☐

6. $12 \times 4 =$ ☐

7. $13 \times 6 =$ ☐

8. $18 \times 9 =$ ☐

9. $24 \times 6 =$ ☐

10. $78 \times 9 =$ ☐

1. 85×10 = ☐

2. 143×4 = ☐

3. 223×5 = ☐

4. 387×8 = ☐

5. 512×9 = ☐

6. 734×7 = ☐

7. 888×6 = ☐

8. 913×4 = ☐

9. 662×9 = ☐

10. 498×8 = ☐

Check your answers.

Answers

Page 6: **1.** 20,22,24 **2.** 84,86,88,90 **3.** 40,42,44
4. 60,62,66,68 **5.** 26,28,30,32

Page 7: **1.** 10 **2.** 6 **3.** 4 **4.** 12 **5.** 8

Page 10: **1.** 9,6,3 **2.** 30,27,24 **3.** 72,69,66,63
4. 63,60,57,54 **5.** 39,36,33

Page 11: **1.** 18 **2.** 6 **3.** 33 **4.** 27 **5.** 30

Page 14: **1.** 4 **2.** 4 **3.** 4 **4.** 4 **5.** 4
6. 12 **7.** 0 **8.** 6 **9.** 9 **10.** 8

Page 15 **1.** 20 **2.** 32 **3.** 48 **4.** 44 **5.** 4

Page 18: **1.** 8 **2.** 5 **3.** 9 **4.** 12 **5.** 4

Page 19: **1.** 30 **2.** 40 **3.** 55 **4.** 0 **5.** 15

Page 22 **1.** 6 **2.** 6 **3.** 6 **4.** 6 **5.** 6
6. 7 **7.** 10 **8.** 9 **9.** 8 **10.** 12

Page 23: **1.** 48,48 **2.** 18,18 **3.** 60,60 **4.** 24,24
5. 72,72

Page 26/27: **1.** 36 **2.** 21 **3.** 2 **4.** 16 **5.** 4 **6.** 49
7. 3 **8.** 20 **9.** 6 **10.** 5 **11.** 5 **12.** 0
13. 24 **14.** 2 **15.** 48

Page 30: **1.** 0 **2.** 32 **3.** 56 **4.** 40 **5.** 96
6. 8 **7.** 0 **8.** 8 **9.** 11 **10.** 8

Page 31: **1.** 48 **2.** 0 **3.** 72 **4.** 96 **5.** 80

Page 34: **1.** 18,27,36 **2.** 63,72 **3.** 72,63
4. 0,18,27 **5.** 27,45,54,63

Page 35: **1.** 45 **2.** 81 **3.** 27 **4.** 54 **5.** 99

Page 38: **1.** 10 **2.** 7 **3.** 5 **4.** 3 **5.** 8
6. 60 **7.** 90 **8.** 110 **9.** 120 **10.** 40

Page 39: **1.** 20,30 **2.** 70,90 **3.** 90,80,70
4. 50,80,90 **5.** 10,20,30

Page 42: **1a.** 12 **1b.** 3 **1c.** 6 **1d.** 9 **1e.** 12
2a. 40 2b. 8 **2c.** 16 **2d.** 24 **2e.** 32 **2f.** 40

Page 43: **3a.** 27 **3b.** 9 **3c.** 18 **3d.** 27 **4a.** 28 **4b.** 7
4c. 14 **4d.** 21 **4e.** 28

Page 44: **1a.** 72 **1b.** 72 **2a.** 55 **2b.** 55 **3a.** 56
3b. 56 **4a.** 24 **4b.** 24

Answers

Page 45: **1a.** 12 **1b.** 24 **1c.** 36 **1d.** 48 **1e.** 60 **1f.** 72 **2a.** 11 **2b.** 22 **2c.** 33 **2d.** 44 **2e.** 55 **3a.** 7 **3b.** 14 **3c.** 21 **3d.** 28 **3e.** 35 **3f.** 42 **3g.** 49 **3h.** 56 **4a.** 8 **4b.** 16 **4c.** 24

Page 46: **1a.** 4 **1b.** 8 **1c.** 12 **1d.** 16 **1e.** 20 **2.** 20 **3a.** 5 **3b.** 10 **3c.** 15 **3d.** 20 **4.** 20

Page 47: **1a.** 7 **1b.** 14 **1c.** 21 **1d.** 28 **1e.** 35 **2.** 35 **3a.** 5 **3b.** 10 **3c.** 15 **3d.** 20 **3e.** 25 **3f.** 30 **3g.** 35 **4.** 35

Page 49: **1.** 8 **2.** 8 **3.** 54 **4.** 28

Page 50: **1.** 14 **2.** 4 **3.** 7 **4.** 5 **5.** 2 **6.** 4 **7.** 40 **8.** 2 **9.** 27 **10.** 7 **11.** 63 **12.** 1

Page 51 **1.** 84 **2.** 9 **3.** 110 **4.** 12 **5.** 35 **6.** 24 **7.** 12 **8.** 24 **9.** 80 **10.** 81

Page 52: **1a.** 77 **1b.** 70 **1c.** 7 **1d.** 77

Page 53: **1a.** 120 **1b.** 100 **1c.** 20 **1d.** 120 **2a.** 135 **2b.** 90 **2c.** 45 **2d.** 135 **3a.** 168 **3b.** 80 **3c.** 80 **3d.** 8 **3e.** 168

Page 55: **1a.** 85 **2.** 90 **3.** 192 **4.** 234 **5.** 162 **6.** 132 **7.** 312 **8.** 294 **9.** 415 **10.** 532

Page 57: **1.** 372 **2.** 835 **3.** 1592 **4.** 1230 **5.** 1264 **6.** 1602 **7.** 3376 **8.** 3829 **9.** 2150 **10.** 1288

Page 58: **1a.** 2056 **1b.** 1600 **1c.** 400 **1d.** 56 **1e.** 2056 **1f.** 2056

Page 59: **1a.** 2772 **1b.** 2100 **1c.** 630 **1d.** 42 **1e.** 2772 **1f.** 2772 **2a.** 2780 **2b.** 2000 **2c.** 700 **2d.** 80 **2e.** 2780 **2f.** 2780

Page 60: **1.** 6 **2.** 56 **3.** 99 **4.** 6 **5.** 8 **6.** 120 **7.** 12 **8.** 7 **9.** 40 **10.** 108

Page 61: **1.** 6 **2.** 8 **3.** 18 **4.** 72 **5.** 108 **6.** 48 **7.** 78 **8.** 162 **9.** 144 **10.** 702

Page 62: **1.** 850 **2.** 572 **3.** 1115 **4.** 3096 **5.** 4608 **6.** 5138 **7.** 5328 **8.** 3652 **9.** 5958 **10.** 3984